MY FIRST REFERENCE LIBRARY

LANDSCAPE

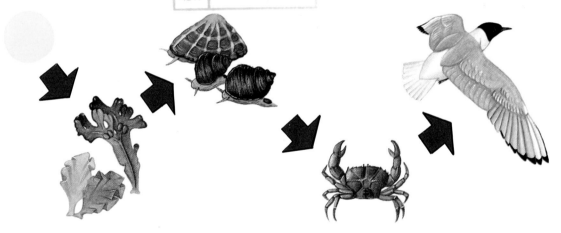

by Robert Brown
Adapted from D.C. Money's
Our Changing Landscape

BELITHA PRESS

First published in Great Britain in 1990 by
Belitha Press Limited
31 Newington Green, London N16 9PU
Copyright © Belitha Press Limited and
Gareth Stevens, Inc. 1990
Illustrations/photographs copyright © in this
format by Belitha Press Limited and Gareth
Stevens, Inc. 1990
ISBN 1 85561 038 8
Typeset by Chambers Wallace, London
Reprinted in 1991 in Hong Kong
for Imago Publishing

British Library Cataloguing in Publication Data
CIP data for this book is available from the British
Library

Acknowledgements

Photographic credits:

N. Champion 7 bottom, 19, 40 left
The Creative Company, Milton Keynes 39
Geoscience Features 5 right
Glenrothes Development Corporation 37
Sally and Richard Greenhill 16
Susan Griggs Agency Ltd 13, 20 bottom, 47, 54
Robert Harding Picture Library 7 top, 30, 31 bottom,
    44, 52, 56, 57
The Hutchinson Library 10, 22, 23 bottom, 26, 28, 32,
    35, 41, 43 left, 46, 49
The Mansell Collection Ltd 23 top, 31 top
D C Money 4, 9, 11, 15, 18, 20 top, 25 top, 29, 33, 34,
    38, 40 right, 45, 51, 59
Marion and Tony Morrison 25 right
Joachim Schumacher 53
Science Photo Library 5 top
Spectrum Colour Library 27, 43 right
Frank Spooner Pictures 50
A. Usborne 21

Illustrated by: Nicholas Day and David Holmes
(Garden Studios), Eugene Fleury, Edward
Mortelmans (John Martins Artists)

Series editors: Neil Champion and Mark Sachner
Educational consultant: Carolyn Kain
Editors: Kate Scarborough and Rita Reitci
Designed by: Groom and Pickerill
Picture research: Ann Usborne

Contents

Words found in **bold** are explained
in the glossary on pages 60 and 61

Earth's Surface

Did you know?

The Earth's surface is more than 4,000 million years old. It is not easy to imagine such a vast amount of time. But in a million years, a river can cut a valley 1,000 m deep.

▼ This stream has cut a deep gulley into a steep mountain in the Andes.

CHAPTER ONE

CHANGING EARTH

The surface of the Earth is always changing. We do not notice many of these natural changes because they take place very slowly over millions of years. Many of the changes people make to the **environment** are easier to see.

Natural forces

Sometimes nature can bring enormous change. In 1980 a volcano called Mt. Saint Helens erupted in Washington, USA. It destroyed many stretches of forests and farms. But most natural changes take place more slowly.

Effects of wind and water erosion

wind-scoured surface

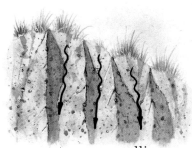

water-worn gullies

Slow changes

The Earth's solid **crust** is divided into separate **plates** that move very slowly. As these huge plates collide, either surface rocks gradually crumple or mountain ranges are forced up. As plates move apart, new oceans may spread. These changes take millions of years. **Erosion** is also a slow process. Wind and water wear down surface rocks. Frost cracks them. Rock grains form new soils. They can make **deltas** where rivers meet the sea.

▲ The explosion from a volcano changes the Earth's surface rapidly. Solid matter builds up the volcano's sides.

▲ Oahu Island is the top of a volcano built up from the bottom of the Pacific Ocean.

▼ Rivers dump sand and mud to form islands and deltas where they open out into the sea.

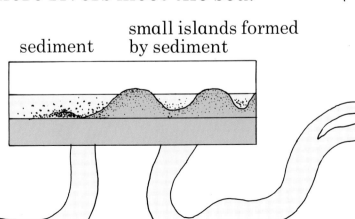

sediment

small islands formed by sediment

river flowing to sea

sea

delta

Change

▶ To help people survive, early settlements needed fresh water, forests, a steady supply of animals for food and clothing, and, later, good soil for growing crops.

Ten thousand years ago, most people lived in small groups. Their ways of life fitted in with nature. In time, these people settled where there were **fertile** soils and water. People started to live along rivers, such

▶ Early settlements grew slowly, because many people did not live long. As settlements got larger, the landscape was changed. People cleared forests for farming. Bridges were built and paths cleared for hunting or travelling.

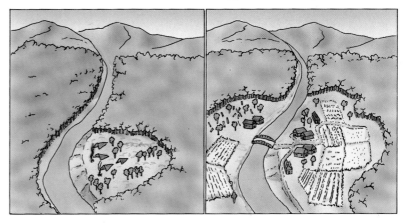

as the Nile in Egypt and the Indus in Pakistan. They used animals, water, and fuels to improve their lives. They built houses, roads, and water channels. This changed the landscape.

▲ The valley of the River Indus was at the centre of one of the earliest great civilizations. Its wide, fertile banks grew food for a great many people. It flows through what is now Pakistan.

◀ The ruins of Rome among modern buildings. Rome grew from a settlement on the banks of the River Tiber, in Italy, and became the splendid centre of a powerful empire.

Pressure on the Landscape

Did you know?

In 9000 BC, there were about five million people living on Earth. Now there are 5,000 million!

Today, five thousand million people live on Earth. This has meant that many more changes have been made to the landscape. Because our population continues to grow, we use more and more land for farms, factories, and cities.

Long-term effects

Sadly, we do not always think of the future. The land, sea and air have all been **polluted**. We destroy many different kinds of plants and animals. Not only trees and large animals suffer, but also tiny creatures. All of this has a bad effect on our environment.

Changing for the better

People change the landscape to improve their way of life. And for many people their way of life has

▶ How the use of the same section of land has changed through the centuries. Left: a castle and a village in the Middle Ages. Centre: factories in the nineteenth century. Right: light industry, modern high-rise flats, and golf course.

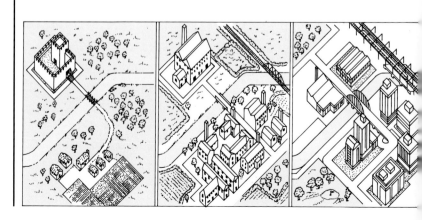

◀ Crowds on their way to work in Xian city in northern China. When Xian was the ancient capital of China, the people lived within the walls of the city. Now millions live here. You can see the chimneys of factories that have spread beyond the old walls. The gate to the old city is shown towering at the end of the road.

got better. Now we need to make sure that we make changes without harming our environment.

▲ In Australia, sulphur fumes from copper smelters have killed the beautiful forests that once covered these hills in Tasmania.

Nature's Balance

CHAPTER TWO

THE WORLD AROUND US

Everywhere living and non-living things affect one another. The Sun affects all aspects of our weather on Earth. The weather can break up rocks. The pieces broken from rocks form the soil that plants grow in. Plants need sunlight, water and **minerals** to grow. They also need to breathe in a gas that is present in the air called carbon dioxide. They breathe out another gas called oxygen. Animals breathe in

Did you know?

In South America, less than half the area of rain forest trees cut down each year is replanted.

▶ Tropical rain forests are full of plant and animal life that depends upon the trees for protection. When the trees are removed, soil washes away in floods, and the land becomes barren. This is happening in huge areas today.

A food chain

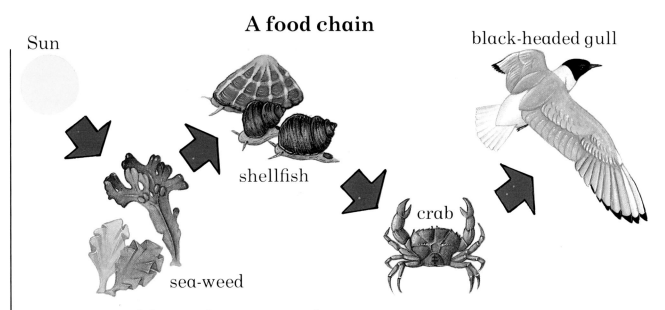

Sun

sea-weed

shellfish

crab

black-headed gull

oxygen and breathe out carbon dioxide. Animals must also either eat plants or other animals so that they can live. The way in which all these different things balance with each other is called an **ecosystem**.

Upsetting the balance

Any change in the ecosystem, such as a lack of water or minerals, can affect all the members of that system. Natural events sometimes change the balance of an ecosystem. Floods and volcanoes can rapidly alter an environment. People can also change the environment and bring about the breakdown of an ecosystem. For example, the building of towns and cities destroys an ecosystem.

▲ These pictures show how energy from the Sun passes along from plants all the way to animals, such as sea birds.

▼ Cattle grazing near Mekele in Ethiopia will return to these walled enclosures. In the dry season when grass does not grow, they eat hay.

Living in Harmony

The Mayas

The Mayan civilization prospered between AD 300 and AD 900. They developed advanced picture writing and numbering systems.

Some **communities** have hardly changed their environment. For example, the Mayan Indians lived in the forests of Central America for thousands of years. They did little to disturb nature's balance. They built wood houses with thatched roofs. They gathered fruits and wild honey, fished in local streams, and hunted.

▶ In the early 16th century, Spanish soldiers came by boat to South America with horses, armour and weapons. They conquered the Mayan people. These soldiers were called the Spanish conquistadors.

Traditional Indian ways

About 100 years ago, outsiders came to these forests. They cut down the **mahogany** trees. Recently, other newcomers began clearing forests for farms, ranches, roads, and airstrips. Now the Mayas live in tin-roofed shacks and eat canned food. Few of them now hunt or fish. Sadly, their traditional ways no longer exist.

▲ The Central American Indians had a very organized way of life. They developed many skills, such as pottery, basketry and sculpture. They built immense stone temples for worshipping their gods.

◄ This Mayan family burns branches to cook. They built their home and furniture out of wood from their surrounding forest. Their clothes come from a local shop.

13

Changing the Landscape

In some places, people have successfully changed the landscape. They have skilfully replaced trees and plants with crops like rice.

Growing needs

Old settlements often fitted into their landscapes. People living in a village surrounded by trees most likely built log cabins. Small groups care about their environment. Until lately, this was true of most market towns. But the world's population is growing fast. Today, most people live in cities. They need food that has to be grown in the country. Most people are not aware that this is changing the countryside.

▼ This house in Switzerland is made from local wood. The snow falls off the steep roof.

14

▲ In Bali people have cut the sloping land into terraces for rice growing.

◄ In Ethiopia, fields follow the shape of volcanic slopes.

The acid rain cycle

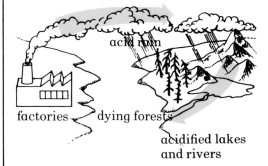

acid rain

factories — dying forests

acidified lakes and rivers

Polluted landscapes

Factories are also changing the landscape. Many factories pour harmful wastes into the water, or into the air to make **acid rain**. This pollutes streams and lakes and harms the living things in them.

Rates of change

Today we can change our landscape rapidly. Earthmoving machines can alter land in hours. Explosives can do it in seconds. Acid rain damage is slow. But its effects are more lasting.

CHAPTER THREE
FARMING

The Land

Farming has greatly changed the world's landscapes. Farmers remove plants that might spoil crops. People have weeded the soil by hand or **harrowed** it ever since farming began. Today chemicals kill unwanted plants.

Growing a single crop year after year keeps taking the same minerals from the soil. When the minerals are used up, the crop fails. So farmers learned to

▼ Today, combine harvesters work in teams to get grain from the huge wheatfields of Kansas. Once these fields were natural open grass land.

rotate crops. A wheat crop that removes nitrogen from the soil is followed by beans or clover that puts it back. Natural and artificial **fertilizers** feed crops. Farmers also breed animals that provide what people want to buy. For example, sheep are bred to have thick wool.

Energy for farming

Farming uses many different forms of energy. The Sun's energy helps plants grow. Human and animal energy sows and harvests crops. Farm machinery, such as tractors and combine harvesters, use fuel. Water and wind turn wheels that make electricity.

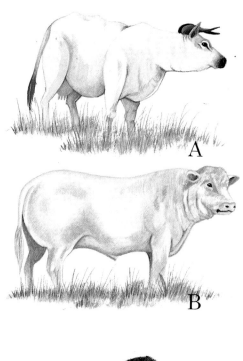
A

B

C

D

▲ Farmers breed native cattle and sheep (A and C) to produce heavy beef cattle and woolly sheep (B and D).

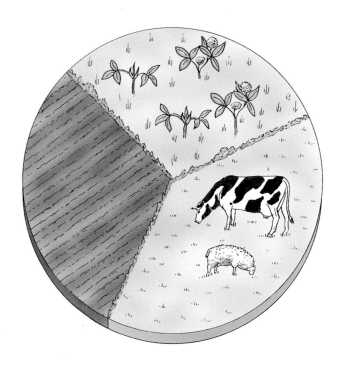

◄ Crops remove nitrogen from the soil, so fields are used in many different ways.

Farm Planning

The farming landscape depends on the kind of land it is and the people who farm it. Some people own land, others rent and some farm in collective groups that share the benefits. In China, a family or a group of villagers agree to cultivate certain areas. They keep some, sell a certain amount to the state, and sell the rest for their own **profit**.

Farming economics

Water affects all farming. Where there is lots of water, it must be carefully controlled. Dry areas need **irrigation**. Without enough water, crops will fail. This causes food shortages and rising food

▼ Farming has changed the hill country of south-west England. Hedges surround some pastures and crops. Old farmhouses and barns shelter in the valley.

prices. In wealthy countries, people can afford higher prices for food. So farmers grow more crops by using irrigation, **insecticides**, and fertilizers. This type of farming is called intensive farming.

▲ In wealthy countries, farmers can afford to hire aircraft to spray fertilizers and pesticides on their land.

▼ Here sheep graze in the valley in North Wales. During the summer, they graze on the hillsides.

Farming for Profit

▼ Modern farming in Cyprus produces fruit and vegetables. They use plastic covers, windmill pumps, trucks, tractors, and fertilizers.

Wool facts

● Australia provides about a quarter of the world's wool supply.

● People have made wool clothes for 12,000 years.

● Australia has over 160 million sheep.

▶ Fencing and irrigation have changed many parts of inland Australia. Once only animals like the kangaroo lived there. Now there are stations (farms) raising millions of sheep.

The farmer runs a business. The landscape works like a factory **producing** crops and animals. The farmer sells these products to make a profit. Some countries sell large amounts of meat, grain and wool to other countries. About 100 years ago, European settlers in North America and Australia started farms. They changed vast stretches of natural grassland to grow grain and keep animals.

Shipping produce

The settlers **exported** and shipped most of the food they grew to Europe. For good crops, they depended on the richness of the soils. But as the soils became less fertile, crop production fell. Today aeroplanes often spray fertilizers. Mechanical equipment is also used, from horse-drawn ploughs to modern combine harvesters. In many farming areas, teams of people move from one farm to another to help with the harvest. The landscape of these areas consists of large fields with **isolated** homes. These farms are connected by long roads and railways.

▲ A farmer in Northern Italy inspects rice before it is sent to Scandinavia. (Top) Far from a rice growing area, a Scandinavian family serves rice shipped from Italy.

Single Crop Farming

A farm where a single crop is grown on a large scale is called a plantation. For the last two centuries, plantations have grown many important crops, such as cotton, rubber, coffee, tea, tobacco, cocoa, and sugar-cane. Plantations replace the natural **vegetation** with rows of carefully tended crops. They have factories to **process** the crops and houses for the workers. In some countries, large areas of land produce a single crop. For instance, in China mulberries are grown to feed silkworms – an ancient practice. Today, silk and cloth factories have changed part of the Chinese landscape.

▼ Women picking leaves on a tea plantation. Tea plantations are found in several countries, like China, Sri Lanka and India.

Plantation farmers must look after the soil. To do this, some use methods that can cause long lasting harm, like artificial fertilizers and pesticides.

▲ This is a 19th century cotton plantation close to the Mississippi River. Until 1865, cotton plantations used slave labour.

◄ Row after row of orange trees show the huge scale of this plantation in California, USA.

Market Towns

▼ This area has many natural advantages.

CHAPTER FOUR

TOWNS AND CITIES

Some country landscapes have stayed the same for a long time. Here, we find villages and towns. As the number of people grow, some villages become towns and some towns become cities.

Living in towns

Towns start up for many reasons. A place may have offered protection, a good supply of water, or minerals. Often, a town grew from a village because it served as a marketplace for farmers to sell their extra crops.

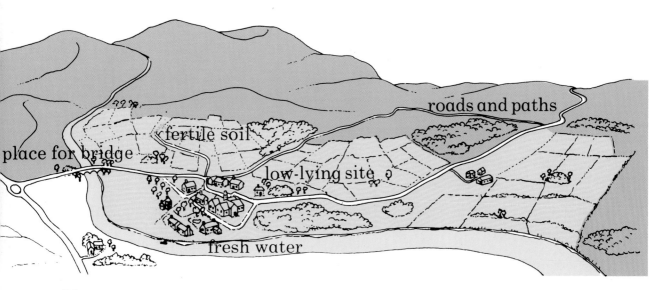

roads and paths

fertile soil

place for bridge

low-lying site

fresh water

Market towns

At busy market towns, many people earn a living by offering services. They may sell food and drink, or repair vehicles. Craftsmen, such as carpenters and blacksmiths, sell their products and services. They build small shops and houses for their families. Larger market towns have hotels, banks and government offices. These towns attract doctors and lawyers.

More recently, some towns have grown because of industry. In the north of England, for example, Sheffield is now a huge town. It grew because it became a centre for the steel industry.

▲ In this small Chinese market town, people from nearby villages gather to sell their produce.

▼ A festival brings crowds to Cuzco in Peru.

Inside a Town

Some parts of a large town may be filled with tall buildings, while other parts may have blocks of flats or houses.

The city centre

In the city centre, there are stores, banks, and government offices. Because land is expensive here, buildings are often tall so they take up less space. Decent housing is very expensive. Large old houses in the city centre are turned into shabby flats in order to squeeze in more people.

▶ Cars help people to travel to shopping centres, where many different shops are close to each other.

From city centre to suburbs

As a city grows, it develops **suburbs**. These suburbs have their own shopping centres, schools, and parks. Since land is often less expensive in the suburbs, people tend to live in houses rather than flats. As the suburbs grow, businesses and factories may come to the area. This is how a city grows and develops a landscape of its own.

▲ Here is a photo of the modern city of Athens. Shops, offices, and tall blocks of flats surround the old Greek town. Suburban housing has spread to the shore and far inland.

Spreading Cities

▼ The poor conditions in a shanty town on the outskirts of São Paolo, Brazil. As housing improves, the government may supply water and electricity. Notice the city centre's high-rise buildings in the background.

In many poorer countries, the number of people living there is growing rapidly. Peasant farmers cannot get more land. As each family grows, their fields become too small to feed them all. Then some of these families move to the city. Some, with little money and no work, build shacks on waste-land and live in these **shanty towns** without sewers, electricity, or running water.

Suburban shanty towns

In poorer countries a city often has a business centre surrounded by busy narrow streets and shops.

◄ In over-crowded cities, young newcomers sell matches, clean shoes, and carry loads.

Nearby there are crowded street markets. On the edge of the city are the home-made shacks of people who are looking for jobs. This kind of suburb is called a shanty town.

▼ Squatter housing on the outskirts of Asunción city in Paraguay is gradually improving.

New Industrial Countries

▼ Super-express trains link many industrial cities of southeast Japan. These trains travel at 220 kph (140 mph).

Several seaports have changed greatly over the past century. For example, Hong Kong and Singapore have become very wealthy ports. They are centres for trade and business. Office buildings tower above business centres. Families live in closely packed high-rise buildings.

Planning urban growth

There are 800 million people living in China's countryside. The **rural** towns encourage light industry, and provide goods and

◀ British ships anchored off Hong Kong Island. The island has belonged to Great Britain since 1842. In 1997, Hong Kong returns to the People's Republic of China.

jobs for local people. Few people move to the cities, so it is these towns that grow. By contrast, on the east coast of the USA, motorways and railways link industrial cities together. Most people in the USA live in cities.

▼ Today, modern high-rise buildings and offices line Hong Kong's western shore. Ocean ships carry goods to and from this busy port.

Buying and Selling

▼ The oceans have many uses in modern business and industry. Ships carry raw materials to factories. Then they distribute the manufactured goods all over the world. Oil tankers deliver fuel to factories. Pipelines from oil platforms, like the one pictured below, carry oil and gas to homes and industries.

CHAPTER FIVE

INDUSTRY AND TRADE

All around the world people make, sell, buy, and **distribute** products. There are three different types of industries. Some people take fish from the sea or oil from the Earth. These are primary industries. Making primary materials into new products is manufacturing industry. People like waiters and dentists and teachers provide services for others. This is service industry.

World trade

Once, people bought and sold produce at local markets. Now, many goods are moved rapidly by truck, ship, train, or plane. Some products, like sugar, are needed worldwide. So in the West Indies and Fiji, for example, sugar cane fields have replaced the natural vegetation. The demand for sugar has changed the landscape of these places.

▲ Many ports have special docks, like the one above in Sydney, Australia. Here, ships can quickly load and unload their goods.

▼ Sugar cane grows on plantations in the West Indies and Fiji.

Industries and Landscape

▼ The effect of any industry depends on its size. This family-owned brick factory in Sri Lanka has made only slight changes to the landscape. They have dug small clay pits and ponds among rubber trees and palms.

Cotton is just one of many products grown all over the world. Many people take part in its growing, packing and shipping. But the making of clothing takes place in different ways. In small workshops hand looms are used. But textile machines need factories. The industrial landscape consists of factories, workers' houses, railways, power stations, and roads.

Raw materials

Taking raw materials for use in factories may affect the landscape. A small brickmaking business may change the environment a little, but a large

a cotton boll

brickmaking company may change the environment for ever. For example, huge areas of Canada's forest are continually being cut down to provide paper for newspapers.

▲ Because of the huge demand for cotton, vast areas are used to grow it. Cotton mills have also changed the landscape.

▶ In Canada, logs float directly to a nearby factory.

Did you know?

Three industry types:

- Primary industry – like farming and mining
- Secondary industry – all manufacturing
- Tertiary industry – services such as police, tourism, and hospitals

35

Different Industries

Manufacturing industries are not all alike. **Heavy industries**, like iron and steel, use large amounts of raw materials. They make **bulky** products, use up a lot of energy, and take up large areas of land.

Light industries

Less bulky materials are used in **light industries**. They make lighter products, such as furniture, processed foods and books. Some light industries use **high technology**. Examples include stereos, TV parts, computers and scientific instruments. These industries are

▼ Metal ores, coal and other minerals are turned into metals by energy and labour in factories. They are later made into other heavy products, such as steel girders.

Heavy industry

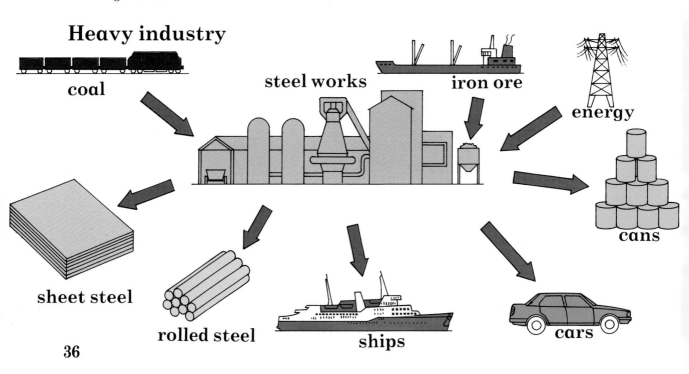

coal

steel works

iron ore

energy

sheet steel

rolled steel

ships

cans

cars

often grouped together. In general, light industries are much less harmful to the environment than heavy industries.

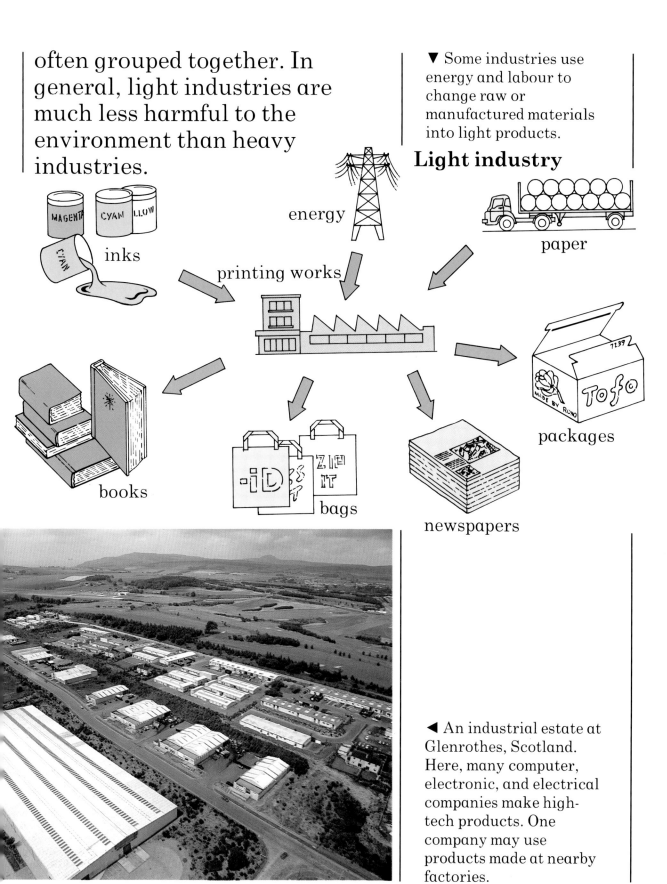

▼ Some industries use energy and labour to change raw or manufactured materials into light products.

Light industry

inks

energy

printing works

paper

books

bags

newspapers

packages

◄ An industrial estate at Glenrothes, Scotland. Here, many computer, electronic, and electrical companies make high-tech products. One company may use products made at nearby factories.

Big Business

Big cities have a central area with many office buildings. These buildings often stand above the rest of the urban landscape. Inside the offices, people buy, sell and trade goods from all over the world.

World traders

Some cities have business centres where people from many countries trade with each other. Hong Kong, for example, is a centre for world business. It is a place where ships crossing the Pacific Ocean load and unload their goods. Hong Kong is home

▼ The central business district of Toronto, looking inland from Lake Ontario.

◀ Light industry and business offices are often on the edges of cities. People, supplies and service equipment can come and go easily, and stay out of the crowded city centres.

to many small industries. Its electronic goods, clothing, jewellery, and other products are sold in thousands of small shops all over the world. It has a high-rise landscape.

▼ Below is a drawing of downtown Toronto. Much of the older housing has been cleared out to build high-rise offices. Most of the workers live outside this area and have to travel in to work daily.

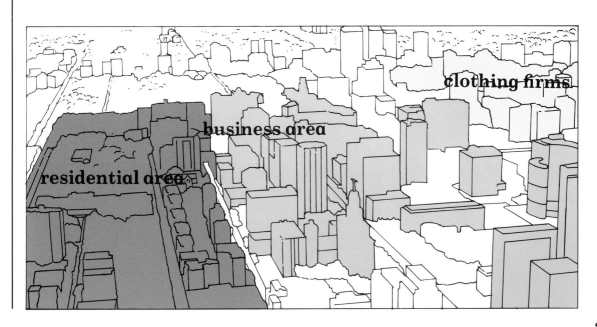

clothing firms

business area

residential area

CHAPTER SIX

TRAVEL

Simple Transport

In many parts of the world, things are still carried on the head or shoulders, strapped to animals, or pushed or pulled on carts. People use pack animals in many countries. Camel trains still carry loads long distances across the sandy Sahara. Yaks and pack horses carry articles over the stony deserts of Central Asia. In India, the ox-cart is still widely used. In poorer countries, animal **transportation** is thought to be cheaper and more reliable than powered vehicles.

▲ Romans paved this path in Wales with flat stones to make walking easier for soldiers.

► This German river valley runs through the wooded hills. It is joined by side valleys – each followed by a road. Roads often follow rivers.

Roads

In country areas, a well-positioned town may become a central market. Well-used roads from the surrounding villages change the environment. With modern travelling methods, market towns now depend on paved roads. For instance, people who live in the Andes mountains depend on good roads. They carry their goods to and from the main road, then crowd into a bus going to the weekly market.

▲ Pack horses are still the best means of carrying loads for the Kirghiz people. They travel through barren, stony mountains west of China.

Canals

The Bridgewater Canal

When the Industrial Revolution began in Great Britain near the end of the 18th century, manufacturers used barges to carry heavy materials like coal and iron ore. Experts built canals for the barges to travel along. One of the earliest was the Bridgewater Canal, built in 1761.

People build canals for boats to carry large and heavy materials. Some canals are vital links. The Saint Lawrence Seaway, for example, joins the Great Lakes of North America to the Atlantic Ocean. Without this canal, large ships would have to unload their **cargo** on the East Coast. It would then have to be carried overland to the Great Lakes region. With the canal, ships can come directly to ports along the Great Lakes.

Inland waterways and ports

Water is a cheap way to carry goods. Canals, like the Suez in

▶ In 1985, the Tennessee-Tombigbee Canal opened. Grain, coal and lumber travel to the Gulf of Mexico along this canal.

Egypt, and the Panama, cut through land to link oceans and seas. A river can also be a valuable transportation route. The Rhine River in Europe, for example, joins sea ports and inland manufacturing areas.

▲ For centuries, the Dutch have used canals to help drain the land and to carry cargo.

▼ Rotterdam is positioned on the North Sea at the mouth of the River Rhine. It is a very important port.

◄ This ship is in the Panama Canal. This canal links the Pacific Ocean to the Caribbean Sea. It is a short cut for many ships.

Transport Networks

In large cities, roads and railways bring in both goods and passengers. Warehouses provide space to stack and load **containers**. In the country, railways and roads may have surprisingly little effect on the landscape. Trees and valleys often hide railway tracks from view. Motorways help take traffic away from minor roads and small towns.

Where routes meet

Passengers and products constantly travel in and out of big cities. Many change from one

▶ Traffic from roads, canals and railways meets at Amsterdam's central station. This canal now provides local transportation, but waterways still link the port with the North Sea.

type of transportation to another – from an aeroplane to a car, or from a lorry to a ship. At certain warehouses, workers split up the contents of large containers. Lorries then deliver the products to widely separated shops.

▲ This photo shows Toronto's harbour on Lake Ontario and its many types of transportation systems. Notice the docks, dockside roads, the motorway and many car parks, the railway tracks, and ships.

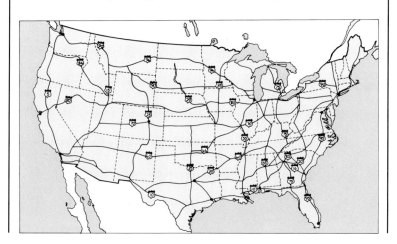

◀ A map of the United States, showing all the states and the main roads that link them. Lorries hauling goods and private cars all depend on this major road network.

Some Bad Effects

People in wealthier countries enjoy many kinds of modern transport. Unfortunately, these also create problems. Rush hour traffic crowds our roads. Cars pollute the air in our cities. Road signs, wires, cables, and billboards make our cities look untidy. Airports take up a lot of space. The noise of aeroplanes disturbs people who live near airports.

Other communications

People can pass on instant messages to each other by the use of telephone, radio, and television. These are called communication networks. Aerials, wires, and cables add to the untidy landscape of our

▼ Crowded city roads are common throughout the world. We are still searching for solutions. Land in cities is scarce and expensive, so building more and bigger roads is not easy.

towns. Many houses now also have small satellite dishes to pick up long-distance television signals.

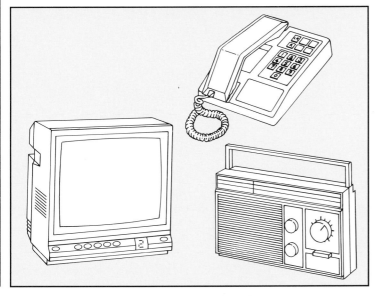

◀ Traffic, mostly yellow cabs, pours into New York's Times Square. People crowd sidewalks. Huge signs advertise consumer products.

▼ A roof-top view of city housing. The aerials, wires and cables allow instant messages to reach our homes through the devices shown opposite.

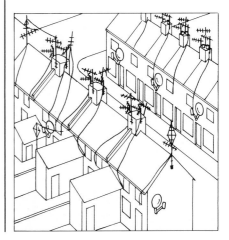

Too Many People

CHAPTER SEVEN

LANDSCAPE UNDER PRESSURE

By the year 2000, there will be over six thousand million people living on Earth. It is the poorer countries where the numbers of people are growing fastest. In these countries there are shortages of housing and food.

People with nowhere to go
In Paraguay, many people lived

▼ This map shows how the numbers of people are growing fastest in the poorer countries. The graph shows how better health care has caused world population to increase.

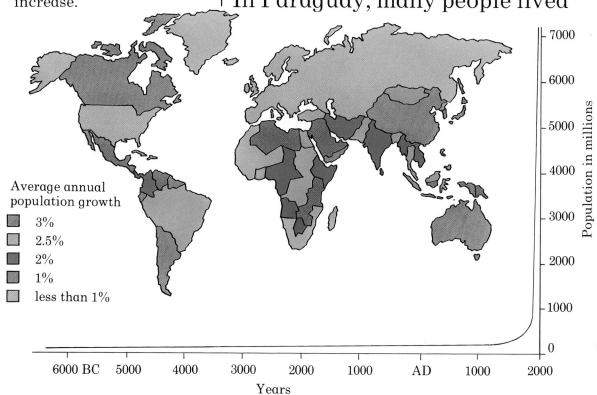

Average annual
population growth
- 3%
- 2.5%
- 2%
- 1%
- less than 1%

Population in millions

7000
6000
5000
4000
3000
2000
1000
0

6000 BC   5000   4000   3000   2000   1000   AD   1000   2000

Years

in the grassy woodlands of the Chaco. Later the settlers from Europe cut down the forests. Now the people of the Chaco have to live in shacks outside Asunción, the capital city. Aborigines of Australia and the Bushmen of Africa's Kalahari Desert also lost their land to settlers from other countries.

▲ This photograph from Hong Kong shows how each family crowds into just a few rooms in this block of flats.

More factories, more waste

The need for more industrial products can harm landscapes. Many factories pollute the air, cause acid rain, and pour out dangerous waste into nearby waters.

Rubbish

In wealthier countries, advertisements convince us to throw out old goods and buy new ones. We demand more new products which use up our natural **resources**. It is not just factories that pollute our environment. We also pollute it with goods and packaging that have been thrown away. Many things we buy, we do not need. Yet millions of people are short of such things as food, clothes and housing.

▼ The rubbish from the rich is picked through by the poor in this South American city.

◄ Packaging adds greatly to our problems of waste disposal.

▼ River barges and wastes from factories pollute the River Rhine in Germany.

The Natural World

Today, people travel far to enjoy natural landscape and wildlife. Sometimes they do not understand how easily they can spoil it. People often leave litter. Their vehicles cut tracks in the soil. Fires, started by accident, can burn forests and farmland.

▼ This flock of goats in Turkey, near the Mediterranean coast, has a few sheep in it. Both sheep and goats can destroy plant cover by nibbling down to the roots. This can ruin the soil and make the land desertlike. ▶

The demand for more farmland threatens natural landscapes. The homes of animals are disturbed and sometimes turned into open zoos.

Relandscaping

Both farming and industrial sites damage the landscape. Abandoned industries leave buildings and dumps behind. Now the governments in some countries help turn these areas into parks and gardens. They do this by tearing down the old structures and **landscaping** the grounds. This can change ugly, disused areas into landscapes that everyone can enjoy.

▲ This used to be an ugly waste dump in Germany's industrial Ruhr. Now it has been turned into a lovely park

▼ The wetlands, like marsh areas, are home to many kinds of wildlife. When people drain these lands, the wildlife disappears.

CHAPTER EIGHT

BECOMING AWARE

Local Problems

We have seen many examples of landscapes being changed in unpleasant or harmful ways. But sometimes when people try to make conditions better, they end up making them worse. Families that move from poor, old housing into new high-rise buildings often feel trapped. They do not like living so far above the ground. For reasons like this, towns should plan their landscapes.

▼ Tall blocks of flats rise from the small houses and the old factories. But in them, some families feel cut off from life in the busy streets below.

A scientific approach

Sometimes scientists can suggest ways of improving farm landscapes. They can find new methods to replace old ones. For instance, planting one crop between another helps prevent soil erosion. The study of wildlife can help many kinds of animals to live in safety. The study and planning of towns is also important to our landscape. There are many people involved in town planning. Those who prepare maps are called surveyors.

◀ The best way to improve our towns and cities is by careful planning. The surveyor (below) helps prepare maps of houses, roads, and gardens, like the one on the left. But others must decide what types of buildings and layouts are best suited for family life.

A land surveyor

theodolite – for measuring angles on the Earth's surface.

A View From Space

Scientists are always looking for new ways to improve the environment and keep it safe. Now they can use aeroplanes and satellites to gather information about Earth's landscape.

Satellites

Satellites move round high above the Earth. They gather a great deal of information about weather, soils, plant life, oceans, and people's activities. Some satellites can pick up and send back television and telephone signals. These satellites stay above the same spot on Earth's surface.

Facts and feats

● A satellite 160 kms (100 miles) above Earth can take a photograph sharp enough to read the words on this page!

● Weather satellites have travelled round Earth since 1960.

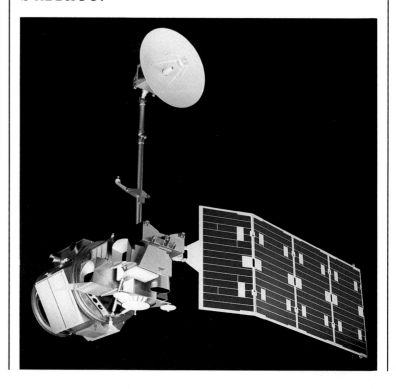

▶ The Landsat-D satellite picks up and sends back information about plants, land use and mineral and water resources.

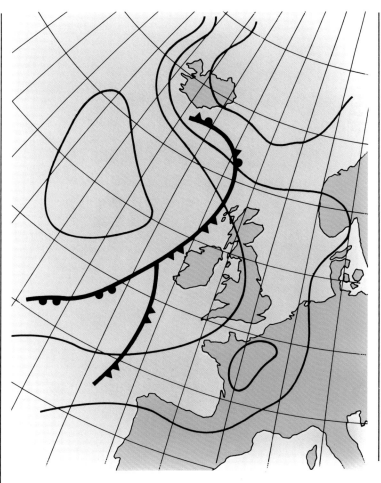

Geostationary orbits

Some satellites move at a speed and direction which allows them to stay above the same spot on Earth's surface. We say they are in geostationary orbits.

◀ A weather map. Information from satellites helps us see weather patterns better than ever before.

▼ Here is a picture sent to Earth by a satellite. It is of North America. The different colours show water and land surfaces.

SPACE PORTRAIT U.S.A.
The First Color Photomosaic of the Contiguous
UNITED STATES
Produced by
GENERAL ELECTRIC COMPANY
Beltsville Photographic Engineering Laboratory
From 569 Landsat Satellite Images
In Cooperation with
The National Geographic Society and
National Aeronautics and Space Administration

Landsat

▶ Satellites circling Earth send back information that helps us understand our world better.

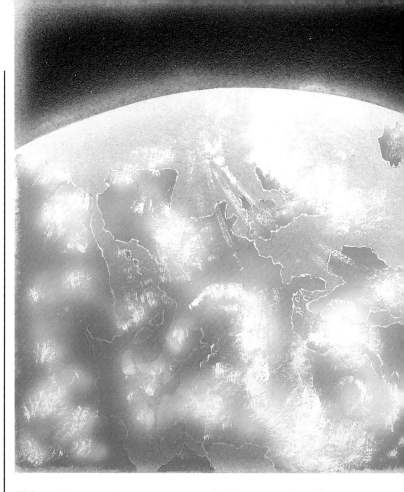

Watching the world

Landsats keep track of:

● Kinds of plant life.

● The amount of pollution in the water.

● The changes in clouds and snow.

● The different types of rock.

● Surface heat levels.

Other satellites track sea resources and weather.

The **Landsat satellites** circle Earth. They go over the North and South poles once every 99 minutes. As the Earth turns beneath the Landsat, it is able to photograph almost the whole surface every 16 days. Each picture it takes shows us different types of rock, soil and vegetation – even plants that grow in the seas!

Seeing landscape changes

Landsat helps us study the Earth's surface. We can watch changes in desert areas, the use of

land, the control of water, the temperature of active volcanoes, the spread of towns. With this information, we can stop or prepare for possible disasters.

◄ The information a Landsat satellite picks up is sent back as a colour picture. It is not the same as a colour photograph. It shows areas where plants grow as red. Towns show up as green. This picture is of the volcano Mount Vesuvius and the Bay of Naples in Italy.

Glossary

Acid rain: this is rain that has been polluted by gases from factories, power stations and cars. These gases turn the rain into acid which causes many water plants and animals to die and trees to lose their leaves.

Bulky: this word describes something that is large and takes up a lot of room.

Cargo: this is the load of goods carried in a ship or aeroplane. The goods can be anything from cars to bananas.

Community: a group of people living close to one another and sharing interests.

Container: a box of a standard size which can be packed with goods. It is easily stacked and moved from one form of transport to another.

Crust: this is a word used to describe the solid surface of the Earth. Underneath the crust, there is very hot and liquid matter.

Delta: this is built up at a certain type of river mouth (the place where a river meets the sea). It has spread out to make a fan shape.

Distribute: this word means to divide or share out between several people or places.

Ecosystem: this word describes a balanced way of life amongst plants, animals and non-living things within a certain area.

Environment: this is a word to describe all the living things, the climate and the kind of land in one particular area.

Erosion: this is a word used to describe the way the land is worn away by the wind or water. For example, cliffs are worn down by both the wind and the sea.

Export: to carry or send out goods from one country to another.

Fertile: an animal or a plant is said to be fertile when it is able to reproduce itself. The soil is said to be fertile when plants grow well in it.

Fertilizers: these are substances that are put on the land by farmers to make the ground better for growing plants and crops. Sometimes they only help for a short time and then they make the ground poisonous.

Harrow: this is a tool used by farmers to break up the ground. When the earth is harrowed, it means that it is being broken up by a harrow.

Heavy industry: a type of industry which produces goods that are sometimes heavy and always large.

High technology: technology describes a way of making any science useful in industry. High technology especially uses the science of electricity.

Insecticides: a substance used to kill insects that might do harm to crops.

Irrigation: this is a word to describe the way people water land that would otherwise be too dry to grow crops in.

Isolate: this word means to set apart or separate. When a village is isolated, it means that it is miles from any other village or town.

Landsat satellite: this is a space craft used to send information about the Earth's surface back to scientists. One was first launched by NASA in the USA in 1972.

Landscape: to lay the land out and make it look better. Landscape is also the word used to describe the actual lay-out of land.

Light industry: an industry where the materials used and the goods produced are light and take up little space.

Mahogany: a rainforest tree with a hard reddish-brown wood. It is often used to make furniture.

Minerals: this is a word to describe substances found naturally in the ground that do not come from animals or plants, such as iron or rock salt.

Plates: the Earth's solid surface is divided up into huge sections, which are called plates. They support whole continents and oceans and are continually moving. Where one plate meets another there is often a huge range of mountains.

Pollute: this is a word to describe the spoiling or poisoning of the world around us. For example, people pollute the sea by dumping rubbish and chemical waste from factories into it.

Process: this word used to describe the set of stages it takes for something to be done or finished.

Produce: anything that has been made or grown is known as produce. To produce means to make or bring forward. The farmer's crop is produced and the crop itself is produce.

Profit: this is a word to describe a gain or benefit. If you sell something for more money than you bought it, the extra money is a profit.

Resources: these are things that can be made use of. For example coal is a resource because it can be made useful when making a fire hot.

Rotate: this is a word used in farming when the crops grown or animals kept in a field are regularly changed. It is very important to rotate crops if you want the soil to stay fertile.

Rural: this is a word to describe anything to do with the country. The opposite to this is urban, which means anything to do with the town.

Shanty town: this is an area of a town which is made up of homes that are roughly made. The people who live there are very poor and cannot afford to live in proper houses.

Suburbs: the outer parts of a town where people live rather than work.

Transportation: this word covers all the different ways that people and goods get around, from aeroplanes to bicycles.

Vegetation: this word describes all the plants that grow naturally. Trees, bushes, grass and flowers are all vegetation.

Index

A number in **bold** shows the entry is illustrated on that page. The same page often has writing about the entry too.